CHRISTIAN
CITIZENSHIP

CHRISTIAN CITIZENSHIP
Mike Morris

WORD

BOOKS

WORD PUBLISHING
Nelson Word Ltd
Milton Keynes, England

WORD AUSTRALIA
Kilsyth, Victoria, Australia

WORD COMMUNICATIONS LTD
Vancouver, B.C., Canada

STRUIK CHRISTIAN BOOKS (PTY) LTD
Cape Town, South Africa

CHRISTIAN MARKETING NEW ZEALAND LTD
Havelock North, New Zealand

JENSCO LTD
Hong Kong

JOINT DISTRIBUTORS SINGAPORE—
ALBY COMMERCIAL ENTERPRISES PTE LTD
and
CAMPUS CRUSADE, ASIA LTD

SALVATION BOOK CENTRE
Malaysia

CHRISTIAN CITIZENSHIP

© Pioneer 1993.

Published by Nelson Word Ltd./Pioneer 1993.

ISBN 0-85009-734-7   (Australia ISBN 1-86258-311-0)

Unless otherwise indicated, Scripture quotations are from the HOLY BIBLE, NEW INTERNATIONAL VERSION (NIV), copyright © 1973, 1978, 1984 by International Bible Society.

Front cover illustration: *Red Vineyards at Arles:* Vincent van Gogh, courtesy of Pushkin Museum, Moscow/Bridgeman Art Library (detail).

Reproduced, printed and bound in Great Britain for Nelson Word Ltd. by Cox and Wyman Ltd., Reading.

93 94 95 96 / 10 9 8 7 6 5 4 3 2 1

FOREWORD

Pioneer *Perspectives* are perhaps more than their title suggests!

They are carefully researched presentations of material, on important issues, appealing to thinking churches, creative leaders and responsible Christians.

Each *Perspective* pioneers in as much as it is at the cutting edge of biblical and theological issues. Each will continue to pioneer with new ideas, concepts and data drawn from Scripture, history and a contemporary understanding of both.

They are perspectives in as much as they aim to be an important contribution to the ongoing debate on issues such as women in ministry and leadership; prophets and prophecy in the church; biblical models of evangelism; integrating and discipling new believers; growing and building local churches and further perspectives on Christ's second coming.

Importantly, these studies use a journal style of presentation, and are written by people who are currently working out the implications of the issues they are writing about, in local churches. This is vital if we are to escape the dangerous fantasy of abstract theology without practical experience. They are not written to contribute to the paralysis of analysis—rather to feed, strengthen, nurture and inform so that we can be equipped to get God's will done, by networking the nations with the gospel using all the resources that are available to us.

God's Word is always an event. How much we thank Him that He has left us an orderly account of what He wants us to believe, how He wants us to live, and what He wants us to do in order to bring heaven to the earth. As we embrace a better understanding of Scripture, rooted in local church, national and international mission, we shall become a part of the great eschatological purpose of bringing back the King—not for a church defeated, cowering and retiring but for one which, despite colossal odds, pressures and persecutions, is faithful to her Lord and His Word. To do that we must 'search the Scriptures' to see if many of these 'new things' are true. I commend these *Perspectives* to you as they are published on a regular basis throughout these coming years.

Gerald Coates
Director Pioneer Trust/Team Leader

Pioneer consists of a team and network of churches, committed to dynamic and effective biblical Christianity.

The national team act as advisers and consultants to churches, which in many cases develop into a partnership with the Pioneer team. These are the churches keen to identify with the theology, philosophy, ethos and purpose of Pioneer. The team have a vigorous youth ministry, church-planting strategy and evangelistic emphasis.

Training courses include Equipped to Lead, Emerging Leaders and the highly successful TIE teams (Training In Evangelism).

Pioneer have also been instrumental in initiating and funding March for Jesus (with Ichthus/YWAM); Jubilee Campaign (for the suffering church worldwide); and ACET (Aids Care Education Training).

ACKNOWLEDGEMENTS

The only reason that I have been able to write this *Perspective* is because of the 'Christian Citizenship' team here at Revelation church. It is in fact dedicated to that original bunch of comrades who joined in this adventure from day one.

Although my name appears as the author, in reality I am merely the scribe recording the details of our journey together. The thinking and action contained herein is the product of us all, working alongside each other while engaged in this vital task.

As a group we are especially grateful to Roger Ellis for believing in us. This must be one of those brave and reckless actions at which posterity will marvel! Also to Gerald Coates who has been a personal encouragement and sees the potential impact of this process across the Pioneer network, and beyond, so clearly.

Most of all we want to thank Chris Seaton for his tireless job as chair. Chasing down and sweeping up are both time-consuming and never high on a list of 'my ten favourite lifetime's activities'.

On a personal note I'm thrilled at the support I've received from family. I guess 'little' Katey has found her way round a computer keyboard whilst Jayne suffers the angst of wondering when my patience will expire.

Finally I must express my appreciation and love to my pulchritudinous partner, Katey. It was she who first socialised me and thereby enabled the thinking, which I do in abundance, to have some context and hence relevance to the world in which we live. Without her careful discipling of my character I would simply be raging in a vacuum. If anything of consequence is achieved it is she who should enjoy the credit. Ultimately she will.

Mike Morris
October 1993

This book is dedicated to

Clive Calver

who has always given me the space to be who I am, proved a faithful and true friend and someone I count as a wonderful Christian comrade and citizen.

CONTENTS

PREFACE

What is meant by 'Christian Citizenship'? Any attempt at a substantive definition is guaranteed to draw critical appraisal and alternative concepts. However, to generate such a discussion amongst evangelical and non-evangelical Christians would be, in my view, an evident service to the church and is therefore to be encouraged.

The following *Perspective* emerges from the thinking and aspirations of a small group of diverse evangelicals living, worshipping and serving together on the south coast of England. All members of Revelation church, they are drawn together out of a common concern to find an effective mechanism for outworking the biblical imperative for the marginalised across society. They continue together in a process which attempts to enable the church to engage with the community in which it finds itself.

For many years of the twentieth century the evangelical church has proved itself strong in profession but weak in practice: a culture defined by words and terminology which is sustained by custodians of truth. This 'literatocracy' have reserved the right to interpret the substantive meaning of this 'official speak' back to the church membership or congregation. In all this the church has increasingly lost touch with the society it is called to serve.

Focusing upon itself, the church grasped the primary responsibility and defined its purpose as applying the truth test to its own membership. In this way cultural behaviour patterns such as drinking, smoking, fashion, music, etc. became confused with the rather more challenging business of following Jesus and being devoted to Him. Expertise was developed in 'quality meetings' and 'professional organisation'. These provided for the felt needs of the membership, but did little to dispense bread for the hungry. As a dealer in the currency of spiritual relevance for a world of turmoil, the church verged on the edge of bankruptcy.

This analysis may appear harsh, but it must be acknowledged before the church can again respond to the call of Christ to be witnesses from Jerusalem to the ends of the earth. The very extent of the challenge entails breaking free of culture in order to address it effectively. A message of social involvement with people, the image bearers of God (with its concomitant challenge to honour the integrity of all God's creation) must be presented to challenge the church to recover its historic, biblical role of 'loving neighbour' as well as 'loving self'.

There is today a rising tide of responsibility and a keen desire to get hands dirty in serving the local community; to serve on no other basis than the fact that Jesus loves people; to serve in order to demonstrate the very compassionate character of Christ; to provide a context for the gospel which people anywhere and in any circumstance can understand; to be obedient to the commission of Jesus as reported in Acts 1:8: 'But you will receive power when the Holy Spirit comes upon you; and you will be my witnesses in Jerusalem, and in all Judea and Samaria, and to the ends of the earth.'

PART ONE

ENVISIONING

CHAPTER 1

INTRODUCTION

The Oxford English Dictionary defines 'citizen' as follows:

1.   An inhabitant of a city or (often) a town; esp. a freeman of a city; a townsman (1514); a civilian (1607).

2.   A member of a state, an enfranchised inhabitant of a country, as opposed to an alien.

It further defines citizenship as:

3.   The position or status of a citizen.

What are we to make of all this? In Philippians 3:20 Paul states: 'But our citizenship is in heaven. And we eagerly await a saviour from there, the Lord Jesus Christ . . . '

Citizenship was clearly understood by Paul. Paul was a Jew, a member of the Sanhedrin, but he was also a Roman citizen. The appeal to his citizenship—the fact that he was born a Roman citizen—was sufficient to alarm the commander who had given orders to have Paul flogged, and to gain him passage to Rome for judgement (Acts 22 and following chapters). Citizenship is powerful. The centurion about to flog Paul and the commander who'd ordered the flogging were well aware that citizens enjoyed rights and privileges. To abuse such privilege illegitimately was dangerous.

In describing Christians as 'citizens of heaven', Paul is not focusing upon some eternal status beyond the grave.

Rather he is acknowledging the reality of the new birth for the believer. In becoming Christians you and I are born citizens of heaven, in the same way as Paul was born a citizen of Rome. In the act of repentance, faith and baptism each one of us is sealed with a new citizenship— citizens of the kingdom of God. As with Paul, our citizenship carries rights, or privileges, and responsibilities, or demands. What do I mean by these rights and responsibilities? Let us first consider rights.

Rights or privileges

A right is generally understood to be an entitlement— something I expect, even something I deserve. Whether it is good service on public transport or correct assessment of social security payments I grow indignant if I feel that my rights are not being upheld. Often we find ourselves abusing company personnel when our argument, if justified, is with the organisation in general rather than a specific, isolated employee.

More often than not we subconsciously assume these rights are personal, individual and private in context. They are for my individual and personal enjoyment. I stand at the centre of a universe of my own creation and account for what is owed to me. One might be forgiven for describing this condition as selfishness. And it has severe consequences. Reflect with me for a moment upon one of these consequences.

A cursory glance at the culture which sustains our British society reveals that it is driven by individualism. Candy-coated with a philosophy of individual opportunity for ease of consumption, it fails to generate any sense of mutual responsibility for sectors of society which are unable to benefit easily from naked opportunity. Indeed, a great gulf of insecurity has been introduced to community relationships since the individual has been educated, both directly and indirectly, to look out for his or her own personal interests.

Even within the church, decisions can be taken on the basis of personal advantage: what will I gain by certain actions? Greater profile? Affirmation? A position of leadership? The whole core of our motivation can easily become reduced to individual gain. This is a corruption of the reality of the rights of citizenship.

There is a personal, private, individual right—Paul's entitlement to a trial in Rome—but also a public dimension to that right. Paul's choice was to raise the stakes for the authorities as the newborn church contended for the gospel. This was for the benefit of the whole church of Christ, to meet for worship and engage in evangelism freely throughout society—the opportunity for individuals to change religion and become Christians. It was not therefore purely a personal motivation, but for the greater benefit of the church.

As citizens of heaven we need the mindset that sees rights in the broader context of the rights of the church; and, broader still, the right for God's perspective to influence society in order to secure a value system which provides a generous, caring society. This is a critical question for Britain today.

Responsibilities or demands

Let us move from rights to responsibilities or demands. As a Roman citizen Paul would have been expected to fulfil certain responsibilities. Today we are also expected to fulfil responsibilities, such as to pay taxes and submit to the law as enacted by Parliament as citizens of the UK. We have a right to expect the government to defend us in time of war; we have a responsibility to sustain an armed force to enable government to engage in war. The question of whether we have a responsibility to bear arms by order of the government (conscription) is an area of some debate. Can the government compel me to infringe my conscience? The conscientious objectors in the so-called First World War took their stance on this point: they felt that the state did not have the power to compel citizens to carry arms in defence of the realm. Their story is one of great suffering as they experienced imprisonment and public derision for the stand they took.[1]

What responsibilities do I then have as an individual citizen? Again, responsibilities in the current cultural context throughout the UK tend to be interpreted and understood within a personal and private context: the responsibility for my family, the children's education and welfare, the maintenance of my house. Simply put, the sphere of personal responsibility tends towards becoming very limited.

However, as with rights, there are very public responsibilities required of the citizen. Society recognises this in part when it promotes local neighbourhood watch schemes, calling residents of an area or street back to a sense of mutual responsibility for each other's property. Unfortunately the motivation in such schemes is principally a selfish desire to keep the outward expression of wealth intact. Do neighbourhood watch schemes operate within cardboard city? Probably informally, but not formally.

In reality, as Edmund Burke wrote:

> For evil to triumph it is only necessary for good men to do nothing.

We cannot enjoy the benefits or rights of citizenship without exercising our concomitant responsibilities. The nature of our society, the quality of our government, both national and local, depends upon how effectively we engage in fulfilling our responsibilities. Often there is no external force to monitor our performance or to coerce us. Rather such action must arise from personal choice; a choice that calls for self-discipline and self-motivation. This, it would appear, is so often lacking.

Jesus fully appreciated such responsibilities as He

---

1. See Caroline Moorehead, *Troublesome People: Enemies of War 1916–1986* (Hamish Hamilton, 1987).

described the realities of and implications for neighbourly love. Increasingly, special interest groups compete for a call upon our citizen's conscience by challenging our responsibility for the environment, education, politics, etc. It is for the citizens of the UK to determine the extent to which they will rise to the challenge of their responsibilities as citizens.

We must also take seriously our responsibilities as citizens of heaven. Unfortunately the celebration of the biblical truth that salvation is for the individual—each person having the capacity to meet with God and enjoy their own, unique personal relationship—has generated an unhelpful and individualistic focus across the evangelical church. The joy of personal salvation, whilst a tremendous fact, can restrict our Christian understanding to personal horizons: caricatured as 'Keep your nose clean and you've got a home in glory land.' An over-emphasis on personal morality has prevented the Christian and hence the church from addressing its responsibilities in carrying out Christ's agenda.

One illustration will suffice. In the massive energy legitimately directed by evangelicals towards defending personal sexual morality, there has been a deafening silence over the fragmentation of the social structure, so that the attendant increase in poverty, violence and relationship breakdown has remained unchallenged. The Bible does not allow us the luxury of choosing either the agendas we feel are important or which we believe we can cope with emotionally or socially. Rather it sets before us God's total agenda. In accepting citizenship of heaven we agree to enjoy the rights and pursue the responsibilities such citizenship entails.

For too long evangelical teaching has overemphasised personal or private morality at the expense of what might be termed public morality. The net result has been a church flowing with the culture of the time and adopting a privatised worldview. Failure to criticise the abiding culture has produced a blindness when it comes to the evangelicals' responsibilities. This is therefore the challenge before the evangelical church today: to recover its sense of vocation in the sphere of social responsibility in the name of Jesus Christ.

Some may question the word 'recover'. However, as I hope to illustrate in this *Perspective,* social responsibility is evident throughout the Scriptures. Suffice it to say here that the early church was challenged and took seriously the responsibility to meet physical need. It is not fanciful to read into Acts 2:47 (' . . . enjoying the favour of all the people . . . ') that the thanks, grace or respect the church enjoyed was related to the way it was literal and tangible good news within the community, by deed as well as by word and miraculous signs.

One has only to recall the impetus behind the various monastic movements throughout the Middle Ages before they lost their vision, and hence their way, or the work of Wesley, Shaftesbury, Wilberforce and Booth[2] to realise how closely social responsibility and the proclamation of the good news are related.

The citizenship of these saints carried with it responsibility for all members of the society to which they presented the gospel. History is littered with such examples which support the thesis of this *Perspective.*

---

2. See D. W. Bebbington, *Evangelism in Modern Britain* (Unwin & Hyman, 1988), A. Skevington Wood, *The Burning Heart. John Wesley:Evangelist* (Paternoster, 1967) and Richard Collier, *The General Next to God* (William Collins and Sons Ltd., 1965) amongst the vast range of literature on these personalities.

CHAPTER 2

BIBLICAL CONTEXT

'Without a vision the people perish.'

Vision

Without a clear objective none of us achieves anything. Without inspiration and motivation (which is itself often generated by inspiration) the quality of the fruit of a congregation's or individual's life is subject to question. It is essential that we receive vision from God.

How we get such vision is less important. For example, we may be those who hear clearly and specifically from God. Or we may be inspired and envisioned by another's call, and commit ourselves to serving the outworking of their God-given vision.

It should also be noted that vision is achieved in incremental steps. There is a journey which must be undertaken which leads towards the full expression of the original vision. The vision provides the destination; without a clear destination the journey may well describe ever-decreasing circles and hence lead to nowhere.

Today many expect the realisation of the vision over a very short timespan. They lack the perseverance and the discipline to continue faithfully, step by step, towards the desired, God-given objective. Therefore there is much that is shallow in the church's ministry and mission. As evangelicals we seem to tire easily; we give ground away to the enemy without a fight; we settle for the appearance of success, such is our appetite for success, when there is very little substance.

The Bible gives innumerable snapshots of God's

people, individually and corporately, persevering in the call to fulfil the vision. God sets the time frame; He requires committed faithfulness from His children. Some aspects of the biblical revelation will only be realised by a sacrificial commitment to recover ground surrendered through an earlier failure.

Such sacrificial commitment only flows from vision. I cannot commit myself, my family, my friends to a desert unless I know where I'm headed; unless I can identify the incremental steps towards that vision; unless I can come before God and tell Him how it hurts, how I feel unjustly treated, how I yearn for the comforts of all I see around me, yet can conclude by reasserting the vision, the reason for the sacrifice, the ultimate purpose for the pain, the incremental steps that measure that journey.

On a trip to Egypt I had the privilege of travelling up to Ismailia on the Suez Canal. The hotel I stayed at was situated on the Bitter Lakes, where it is thought by a good number of scholars that Moses crossed the Red Sea with the Israelites.

A number of us from the conference I was attending took a trip around the area one day and crossed the Suez by ferry to step onto the Sinai desert. The contrast that short five-minute journey provided was stunning. The green was left behind for the oceans of sand which was the Sinai. The change was immediate and extreme. One could understand the Israelites complaining to Moses even though they had just experienced the miracle of the Red Sea crossing. What was there to compare with the Egypt they had just left? How would such acres of desert support them?

Joshua later set up monuments of stone at Gilgal, once they had crossed the Jordan. This was to mark an important incremental step in the Israelites' journey from wilderness to Promised Land. Their purpose is explained in Joshua 4:21–24. They were to act as a marker, a reminder to future generations of all that God had done: that they were on a journey and caught up in a vision but that God was the author of that vision and would bring about its fulfilment if the people remained faithful whatever the cost.

Health warning

The need for vision is paramount. This is true in the whole area of our citizen's responsibilities—more especially our responsibility to people whatever situation they (and we) find themselves in.

I want to take the rest of this chapter and the next to establish from the Bible that God has an overriding concern for people, and that this concern should be our concern as sisters and brothers of Jesus and citizens of heaven. Such a concern requires a clear public expression.

For such an expression we need vision and to deliver such a vision demands sacrificial perseverance. Unless we lay hold of this vision personally, and prayerfully commit ourselves as congregations to serve it, Satan will continue to wreak havoc across our society unhindered and unchallenged. So the following carries a heavenly health warning: reading on may seriously disturb your life!

Creation

From the opening pages of the Bible we discover God's heart for mankind. The crown of His creation was humanity—male and female (Gen. 1:26–31). The indelible imprint of God is on every person you see. This alone sets a high value upon humanity. We are to regard all people as priceless. They bear God's image. They are to be treated with great respect. We are to acknowledge that likeness to God, and our behaviour towards each other should always be informed by such an understanding.

Furthermore, God takes personal responsibility for the crown of His creation—advising on how to live, making provision for a full life, detailing rights and responsibilities (Gen. 1:28–30 and Gen. 2:15–25). Every social community demands parameters. God gives such parameters to Eden and its inhabitants.

However, Adam and Eve are tested and found wanting in the area of their responsibilities as citizens of Eden. They choose to follow their own inclination. They elect to pursue a personal agenda for apparent private advantage. They neither refrain from their inclination nor seek counsel from God. The reward is a gain of knowledge, as they had been promised, but a loss of their citizenship. Attempts to disguise the action (Gen. 3:10) are both pitiful and insufficient to recover citizenship.

It is evident that there are clear, tangible consequences to each failure to fulfil the rights and responsibilities equation which accompanies citizenship. With this failure there are broader consequences for the whole of creation (Gen. 3:14–24). When the rights and responsibilities of the Christian citizen are neglected then the effects are felt far more widely than simply the personal impact upon the individual. Our thinking is again so focused upon 'me'— the individual, the self—that we fail to see our personal failure to the whole of God's created order. This created order includes all of the creator rights as given by the Creator. Hence our concerns are not just limited to the concerns of God's image bearers alone. It is at this point we see the unique and essential role for the church in what has been termed the 'green' agenda: environmental issues. We would be failing in our citizenship not to take this broad agenda seriously.[1]

Cain and Abel

Let us move from the creation narratives to the story of Cain and Abel (Gen. 4). In this passage we discover how

---

1. See Chris Seaton, *Whose Earth?* (Crossway Books, 1992).

seriously God considers His image in humankind. For when Cain murders Abel out of jealousy, God calls him to account. The fact that Cain responds to God's question demonstrates that he recognises his responsibility to God. He is accountable to his creator for part of the creation: his brother.

Cain's immediate response is helpful in learning about a citizen of heaven's responsibilities. 'Am I my brother's keeper?' he asks. God replies in the affirmative. Regardless of circumstance Cain is expected to give account to God for his action. Ultimately it is to God that he is responsible. All actions can only be legitimised by God.

When some challenge the basis for evangelical involvement in human rights issues it is to this passage that we must turn. It is not any inherent right enjoyed by an individual that demands we take action or speak out as the church. Rather it is that we realise we have been invested with the responsibility of acting as 'our brother's keeper'. We must answer the question God put to Cain: 'Where is your brother?' It is to the Almighty that we are accountable and we will need to answer this question at the point of judgement.

Wisdom suggests we adopt the position of addressing it now. The church should take up responsibility for all those image bearers of God on the face of the earth. This is neighbourly love in practice—neighbourly love which is addressed in the Old Testament as well as in the New Testament: 'Do not pervert justice; do not show partiality to the poor or favouritism to the great, but judge your neighbour fairly. Do not go about spreading slander among your people' (Leviticus 19:15–16).

Of course not one of us, individually or congregation-ally, can address this question with regard to all the problems in a sin-sick world. Yet recognising the function of vision and the strategy of incremental steps, we start appropriately on our own doorstep. We don't comfort ourselves by celebrating the fact that we are effective within the current membership of our congregation. Rather we lift up our heads, gaze around our local community and listen to the voice of God addressing this critical question on behalf of the community. More of this practice later. All of this foreshadows Jesus' teaching in Matthew 25; yet a further illustration of the harmony between the Old and New Testaments.

Exodus

We now turn to the Exodus of Israel from Egypt, pausing briefly to note God's compassionate heart for Hagar and Ishmael (Gen. 21:15–21). This provides yet another illustration of responsibility neglected this time by Abraham and Sarah. Yet God underwrites the situation, expressing in tangible terms His compassion for these image bearers and their unjust sufferings.

The unjust sufferings of Israel at the hands of the Egyptians lead to God's strategy for leading His people out of Egypt (Exodus 2:23–25). God was concerned for His people. He heard their cry and responded to their plight. God took a man, envisioned him and then by incremental steps accomplished His purpose.

This vision was a subdirectory of the original plan and purpose of God. It got His people back on track, moving the divine plan forward. Because of sin there is continual need for such subdirectories to recover the purposes of God.

It is interesting to note that throughout the process that eventually led to the crossing of the Red Sea and release from oppression, God re-established the rights and responsibilities of citizenship. Obedience to His process culminated in the instructions for the Passover (Exodus 12).[2] Deliverance was dependent upon meeting God's criteria. Citizenship was on His terms.

---

2. Note Exodus 12:43–44 where all non-Israelites were excluded from this specific act of consecration. However such exclusion in no way jeopardised their welfare or the very strong commitment God was to reveal to the Jews in the law for the poor, characterised by the widow, orphan and alien. For us today there may be activities which form part of our evangelical practice which are inappropriate for nonevangelicals. However this does not release us from a commitment to serve and care for them as fellow image bearers of God.

The poor in the Old Testament

When God gave the law to Israel He made clear provision for those who may find themselves on the margins of society. He constantly reminded Israel of their bitter experience as slaves in Egypt and how such remembrance should cause compassion and concern to rise within. This compassionate concern was expected to be expressed in tangible ways—God did not intend the Hagar/Ishmael model to be the norm but rather the exception. Those who knew God and were known by Him, those who reflected His character and advanced His purposes on the earth, these were the ones with the responsibility for the potentially marginalised who should demonstrate the nature of God's kingdom.

Leviticus 19:9–10 reveals God concerned about the economic interests of the poor and the alien:

> When you reap the harvest of your land, do not reap to the very edges of your field or gather the gleanings of your harvest. Do not go over your vineyard a second time or pick up the grapes that have fallen. Leave them for the poor and the alien. I am the LORD your God.

There is a clear prohibition against greed and recognition of how in an agrarian economy the poor can be sustained by that economy without special provisions. Again, verse 15 of the same chapter expresses an unequivocal call to justice—an instruction that all should enjoy equal status before the law and a concern that legal structures should not be weighted in favour of any group: 'Do not pervert justice; do not show partiality to the poor or favouritism to the great, but judge your neighbour fairly.' Finally, verse 33 has much to say to a resident population's reaction to the immigrant: 'When an alien lives with you in your land, do not ill-treat him.' In an age of tremendous people movements, sometimes by chance but more often by war, famine or similar disaster, this is one injunction which strikes at the heart of how we order our lives today. There is a burden of responsibility upon the so-called Western, Northern, economically richer countries.

When verses 15 and 33 are held in tension we must inspect how well the one (v. 33) informs the other (v. 15). There could be some important discussions waiting to be had on nationality and immigration legislation within Britain.

Again, at a broader level there needs to be some theological consideration of the response of the global community to displaced peoples or refugees. This is a critical issue in these final years of the twentieth century, an issue which will continue to challenge us well into the twenty-first!

This principle of the various revelations of God informing each other is essential in seeking a full understanding of the rights and responsibilities of the follower of Jesus, the servant of God.

Consider Deuteronomy 24:12–15 and 17–22:

If the man is poor, do not go to sleep with his pledge in your possession. Return his cloak to him by sunset so that he may sleep in it. Then he will thank you, and it will be regarded as a righteous act in the sight of the LORD your God.

Do not take advantage of a hired man who is poor and needy, whether he is a brother Israelite or an alien living in one of your towns. Pay him his wages each day before sunset, because he is poor and is counting on it. Otherwise he may cry to the LORD against you, and you will be guilty of sin.

Do not deprive the alien or the fatherless of justice, or take the cloak of the widow as a pledge. Remember that you were slaves in Egypt and the LORD your God redeemed you from there. That is why I command you to do this.

When you are harvesting in your field and you overlook a sheaf, do not go back to get it. Leave it for the alien, the fatherless and the widow, so that the LORD your God may bless you in all the work of your hands. When you beat the olives from your trees, do not go over the branches a second time. Leave what remains for the alien, the fatherless and the widow. When you harvest the grapes in your vineyard, do not go over the vines again. Leave what remains for the alien, the fatherless and the widow. Remember that you were slaves in Egypt. That is why I command you to do this.

The same concern for the poor and the marginalised is highlighted. God's people have been entrusted with the responsibility for the way the local community (micro) and society (macro) handles its relations with the marginalised. If society adopts a process which is detrimental to those on the margins, then the church (the congregation which is set within the context of the local community and which finds its validity in the extent to which it interfaces with that local community) must act in accordance with God's revelation, not society's assumptions.

This demands constant vigilance on the part of the church. It must avoid conforming to society's norms. The commitment of the congregation to the marginalised is unavoidable: as God continues faithful in His commitment to His crown of creation, so we must maintain our commitment. I think it is best encapsulated in Ruth's statement to Naomi (Ruth 1:16), in effect, 'We are inseparable.' What that says is, 'My interests are tied to your situation. I cannot elect to take what appears a personally more beneficial route.'

Jubilee

Although the concern for the marginalised is expressed continually throughout Scripture, it is in Leviticus 25 (also Deuteronomy 15) that the heart of it is encapsulated. Principles are laid down, within the context of an agrarian economy, for a just and equitable society. Leviticus speaks of conditions relating to the Sabbath (seventh) year and the year of Jubilee (the consecration of the fiftieth year). Deuteronomy speaks of the Sabbath year alone.

The principle outlined in both Sabbath and Jubilee is that there has to be a mechanism to regulate the accumulation of wealth in the hands of an ever-smaller minority. Recognising that people's economic and social conditions may deteriorate due to their own foolishness, bad management and sin as well as natural catastrophes and injustice, God institutes a balancing-up mechanism so that society might continue to organise itself effectively for its members.

Some might charge that this seems to indicate a naive form of communism. On the contrary, however, I believe it is rather a concern to create a society that is people-focused. Those bearing the image of God become the purpose as well as the constant of society. If society fails to be of benefit to its members, what useful purpose can there be for such a society? On what basis should such a society enjoy the support of its members?

If the aspirations of only one section of society are met, such a society is surely guilty of injustice. Although individual and household fortunes vary, and sin is at work throughout social relationships to create further disorder and disadvantage economically, socially, physically, emotionally and psychologically, there has to be an active commitment to redress the sin factor. Obviously the key is salvation; yet it is what one might call 'informed' salvation—a salvation embracing the concomitant rights and responsibilities of all citizens of the King of kings, a salvation free from a stereotypical model for the recipients of salvation to conform to.

Some might be inclined to argue that Sabbath and Jubilee apply to the people of Israel as a nation chosen by God. With the loss of that role and identity together with the emergence of the new Israel, disciples of Jesus, the implications of such teachings are to practise such principles within the family of God. It is surely the community created by the church which should look after its own membership. This is an excellent starting point for congregations and networks of congregations, as is probably implied by Philippians 2:3–4: 'Do nothing out of selfish ambition or vain conceit, but in humility consider others better than yourselves. Each of you should look not only to your own interests, but also to the interests of others.' However, it is insufficient of itself.

Jesus' parable of the Good Samaritan defines 'neighbour' as the one outside your natural religious community; Samaritans didn't relate to Jews and vice versa. If the greatest two commandments are love for God and neighbour (Matt. 22:37–39) then 'neighbour' cannot be restricted to the Christian brother or sister.

I believe the principle clearly challenges us at the level of our understanding of God's demands for His followers—perhaps more acutely in the context of our Western, materialistic society where an inordinate desire to possess has set itself up as an idol. The sin of worshipping this idol is out of control within many of us. We are instructed to bring self under self-control: 'The fruit of the Spirit is love, joy, peace, patience, kindness, goodness, faithfulness, gentleness and self-control' (Gal. 5:22–23). This is a component of the fruit of the Spirit and so available to all Christians. The challenge before the church is to resist the drive for self-satisfaction.

It is worth noting, in passing, that it is not individual drive and energy which are in themselves sinful, but rather the efforts expended in seeking benefits illegitimately, at the expense of others. Such others are often not very visible by virtue of being on the margins of society. God is calling us back to vigilance. The fruit of such vigilance is in sustaining a lifestyle which approximates to God's revelation and that incarnated by Jesus.

Prophets

Continuing this lightning biblical overview, it is worth

recalling the severe utterances of the prophets at the ill-treatment of people by the chosen people Israel. God fiercely condemns exploitation and injustice in His criticism of the walk and witness of His chosen people and identifies judgement as the consequence of such behaviour.

> When you spread out your hands in prayer,
>> I will hide my eyes from you;
> even if you offer many prayers,
>> I will not listen.
> Your hands are full of blood;
>> wash and make yourselves clean.
> Take your evil deeds
>> out of my sight!
> Stop doing wrong,
>> learn to do right!
> Seek justice,
>> encourage the oppressed.
> Defend the cause of the fatherless,
>> plead the case of the widow.
>>>>>> (Isaiah 1:15–17)

> The LORD takes his place in court;
>> he rises to judge the people.
> The LORD enters into judgement
>> against the elders and leaders of his people:
> 'It is you who have ruined my vineyard:
>> the plunder from the poor is in your houses.
> What do you mean by crushing my people
>> and grinding the faces of the poor?'
>>>> declares the Lord, the LORD Almighty.
>>>>>> (Isaiah 3:13–15)

Isaiah 58:1–14 is another passage which clearly identifies God's perspective. Judgement can only be averted by true repentance. Such repentance is measurable—a different set of standards is adopted and there is a clear change of behaviour.

Amos also hammers the complacent wealth of the

minority, sustaining themselves at the expense of the poor, who are ruthlessly exploited as a result. This word was from God to the people of Israel; it was the heart of the prophetic, comforting only in as far as it revealed a God concerned enough to give public warnings and opportunities for behaviour to be amended before discipline was applied.

Nehemiah

A cameo of God's concern for social justice is provided in the story of Nehemiah. Called by God to rebuild the walls of Jerusalem, Nehemiah, through prayer and careful planning, succeeded against considerable opposition. In the course of carrying out his plan he is made aware that some who were involved in this enterprise were suffering severe financial problems.

The nobles and officials were charging interest on money borrowed by households to buy food. They had no means of supporting themselves, for their land was mortgaged, often to the same nobles. Nehemiah angrily reminds everyone that this is displeasing to God and pleads the cause of the poor. Interest payments are banned. This action is taken before God and with the priests officiating.

Nehemiah recognises the relationship between this economic and physical issue and the spiritual endeavour of completing the walls. We too must recover a sense of the way economics relates to the spiritual agenda. With a holistic worldview we cannot separate so-called spiritual issues from other areas.

It is our task as evangelicals to fulfil our calling in presenting true good news for all. We must not hesitate to challenge injustice wherever we identify it, and to work for its removal at whatever cost and in the face of whatever opposition. Only in this way can we demonstrate that the good news is truly good for everyone.

CHAPTER 3

NEW TESTAMENT AND CITIZENSHIP

The Bible provides us with a harmonious revelation from God. What God reveals in the Old Testament is explained through the New Testament. Hence we discover the concerns for justice so evident in the Old Testament strongly reflected again throughout the New.

The greatest commandment

In Matthew 22:37 Jesus states:

> 'Love the Lord your God with all your heart and with all your soul and with all your mind.' This is the first and greatest commandment. And the second is like it: 'Love your neighbour as yourself.' All the Law and the Prophets hang on these two commandments.

Here he sets out the two greatest commandments. This provides both the vertical and the horizontal dimensions of Christian life and witness—a personal, direct relationship with God Himself, and an all-embracing concern for God's image bearers, fellow travellers with us on this earth.

It has often been illustrated with reference to Calvary and Jesus' death on the cross, which means: the sin problem dealt with; separation between God and man removed; an opportunity for sinful, guilty, confused, disoriented women and men to recover their relationship with God through repentance and faith. This is God's initiative in Jesus, calling for a response from the crown of His creation to the extravagance of His love. This is the vertical dimension.

Yet there is an equally essential and exciting horizontal dynamic: God expressing His concern for the welfare of all humanity—'God so loved the world that WHOSOEVER . . . '! This welfare is only fully met through salvation, but a salvation that addresses every aspect of a person's life. This is the God for the whosoevers, not for a religious élite alone.

This dimension is characterised by the conversation with a crucified criminal calling upon Jesus, hence calling on God, for mercy—mercy freely granted, on the basis of recognition of the reality of who Jesus is.

We are called to love God most definitely, love Him exclusively, passionately, personally; and yet also to live lives with outstretched arms as a sign of welcome and acceptance to all. We are called to embrace all, whosoever they may be.

The record of Jesus' dialogue with the crucified criminals may lead some to conclude that it is exclusively a *spiritual* wellbeing that is both God's and hence the church's concern. However, such an understanding is found wanting at two levels.

In the first place, to force life somehow into two categories, one called spiritual and the other called physical or material, is itself to do violence to the biblical revelation. Once I am saved, *all* of me is saved. I live as a saved individual in every aspect of my life. Whether at a worship meeting or shopping in the supermarket I am an evangelical. I am no more an evangelical in the former context than in the latter. The attitudes and actions displayed in the supermarket should not be at variance with those displayed in the worship meeting.

Unfortunately, too often the church has been dictated to by society's prevailing mores. It has failed to recognise that our knowledge of God is for application to the whole of life. Too often the church has failed to resist the pressure of the ascendant patterns and customs prevalent across everyday society. We should, however, realise that *everything* we do, experience or are subject to is to be confronted and influenced by the spirit of God and done to the glory of God. What is my attitude and behaviour to the traffic policeman who stops me for speeding? Anger? Irritation? Am I abusive? Short-tempered in my conversation with him? Do I lie in the hope of avoiding a penalty? Do I seek to prevent the fact that I have been stopped from becoming public knowledge through shame, or some sense that it is 'not very Christian'?

If I face injustice individually or as part of a group I am called to respond with an attitude and with actions that carry the hallmark of Jesus. This does not preclude the addressing and exposure of the evil. However, it does require a distinctive attitude that is clearly modelled on Jesus. On the other hand, if I am part of the group which enjoys all the benefits of society, then I must not fail to identify injustice and also resist profiting at the expense of others. Complacency or ignorance are not valid positions for the evangelical who seeks to live a biblical lifestyle.

The Good Samaritan

Secondly, the view that the church should be concerned solely or principally with people's *spiritual* wellbeing is at variance with Jesus' own teaching on neighbourly love, as reflected in the story of the Good Samaritan. In response to a question about the identity of one's neighbour, Jesus indicates that it is whoever is in need. The story Jesus tells reflects a racial and cultural conflict; yet as a parable it enshrines principles that must be applied broadly across society. These principles apply literally to anyone who, in our estimation, meets the criteria. This allows for very few, if any, exclusions!

Note that the Samaritan set aside his prejudices, unlike the earlier Jewish travellers who had ignored the injured man's plight. In doing this the Samaritan also had to risk being misunderstood and possibly rejected by his own racial group. There was also the possibility that the injured Jew would refuse his help, on similar racist grounds.

Also noteworthy is the way that the Samaritan allowed his own schedule to be interrupted. He was prepared to be inconvenienced. Today, in our age of time management and the desire for a measurable return from time invested, our time and the use of it is one of the most sacred areas of life. In loving our neighbours we need to recognise that there will be a measurable impact upon our self-styled schedule, agenda and business or home life. Involvement has clear consequences. The Samaritan went further in committing personal financial resources to meet the human need he was confronted with. Again, this was both for the immediate and the medium-term treatment. In our financially anxious society it is a measure of where our heart lies as to how loosely we hold to our income and savings.

On another occasion Jesus picked up on the relationship between one's material wellbeing and love of God. In Matthew 6:19–24 He declares that it is impossible to serve two masters. Only one master is suitable for the disciple. However the reality of the service we give to God is measured by what we are investing in. This may not be overt investment, but it is where our security lies. What is the focus of our aspirations? Where is our 'heart'? If we are to prove effective in serving God then our full affection must be given to Him. We must break with our Western materialistic model, with its security built upon financial wellbeing, and make all that we have available to God.

The question of 'how?' often arises. The first of a number of incremental steps would be to ensure that all income is tithed gross. That is, ten per cent of everything earned before tax is invested directly in the work of God, usually through the local church. Of course this percentage grows with the level of income. The only way to ensure it does, is to determine a level of lifestyle that one is to practise and then budget for it honestly. The excess income over budgeted expenditure is then available directly to God. We also resist the pressure of impulse buying, or replacing things because of advancing technology, because to do so lies outside our budget. In this way we (the church), like the Samaritan, should release resources for the care of neighbours in society.

People who are on income support, unemployment benefit, etc. could rightly say this excludes them, as they have no surplus. I agree. However, if we are part of the church then energy and time, matched with the flow of finances across the congregation, produces a potent mix of resourced people to care for neighbours within the community. Furthermore, there is a much-needed debate on how we should be living as congregations; the extent of our households; what we are modelling as family; the mechanisms we are deploying to empower the financially vulnerable as equal members of God's church.

In identifying neighbourly love as the second most important command, and then describing who our neighbour is, Jesus has set before the church a reasonable responsibility for involvement in community care—a practical, intense and tangible care. The church must identify and live practically alongside its neighbours as defined above, within the community it seeks to minister to. I guarantee that there is no shortage of candidates for such neighbourly love. What is lacking, I would suggest, is an effective strategy regarding time and resources to meet the challenge and opportunity of serving in this horizontal plain.

Sheep and goats

Perhaps the clearest implications of this vertical/horizontal matrix are found in Jesus' words as recorded in Matthew 25. Here a clear picture of judgement is presented. It is a judgement which links practical performance on the social agenda with supernatural ministry in the spiritual agenda. The chapter demonstrates once again the ludicrous position of seeking to separate the spiritual and the practical in reality. They are indivisibly joined.

In spite of a remarkable supernatural ministry Jesus dismisses a group of people, apparent followers, for failure to attend to such practicalities as prison visitation, handing out cups of water, etc. It is perhaps a hard passage to appreciate at first, for it would appear to trespass upon the doctrine of justification by faith alone. However it is supported by other passages, such as the epistle of James, as we shall see later. Furthermore, it reflects the concerns presented throughout the Old Testament, as we have already noted. What all such passages do is to unpack the meaning and indicate the nature of justification by faith, rather than do damage to it.

Judgement evidently does owe something to the way we have exercised our rights and responsibilities as Christian citizens. We must apply ourselves to explore the precise nature of this relationship between personal devotion to Jesus, and a realistic concern for those with needs across our communities, especially those whose needs are not well catered for by existing societal structures.

This relationship must be explored in more than just words; consultations, symposia and processes have their place, but often occupy the high ground alone. This whole *Perspective* is a compilation of further words; the challenge to my household and to all who read it is to initiate *practical outworkings* of the substance. We require far more models established to demonstrate the truth of our words and the validity of the good news.

Early church

In the first years of the church, following the death, resurrection and ascension of Jesus, a principle of mutual responsibility was adopted. Inspired by the Holy Spirit from Pentecost onwards, the church was bold in its verbal and lifestyle proclamation of the gospel. This had an incredible impact upon the local population, as the growth statistics confirm!

The best description that I have found for the amazing lifestyle of the early disciples as they pioneered church is found in Ronald Sider's book, *Rich Christians in an Age of Hunger*.[1] He writes:

> Oneness in Christ for the earliest Christian community meant *unlimited economic liability for, and total economic availability to*, the other members of Christ's body.

The Jerusalem church from the start practised unlimited economic liability and total economic availability. The harsh judgement on Ananias and Sapphira (Acts 5:1–11) reflects the priority this had on God's agenda.

We might not want to use the adjective 'economic', since it is a limiting agent. We should exercise such unlimited liability and total availability in every area of life. However, since money and material possessions have so strong a grip upon Western society at present, it is appropriate to highlight it. If this economic issue alone was addressed, the impact across the church would be incredible.

The open house lifestyle mentioned in the two snapshots of the early church given to us (Acts 2:42–46 and Acts 4:32–37) teaches us a lot. Unfortunately most biblical interpretation available to us has historically been approached from a Western cultural setting. Yet the Bible is located historically in a Middle Eastern setting, and the so-called 'radical' households depicted here are probably reflecting Middle Eastern culture.

However there are clear principles which confirm the picture we have been building biblically throughout this *Perspective*. The responsibility to engage in a holistic

---

1. Hodder and Stoughton, 1978. Quote from p. 91 of 1979 paperback edition.

approach is assumed; praying and eating and meeting needs are intertwined and in fact the norm of Christian life.

Worth noting as well is the fact that if this unlimited liability and total availability is operating across the church, then the ability of the church to act effectively within the community is enhanced many times over. The resources available are multiplied. The capacity of an interactive group is far more flexible and stronger than that of one or two individuals. In this way the church again demonstrates the spectrum of gifting operational within the body of Christ and presents a truer picture of God at work in the world today.

James

In the epistle of James the implications of works as an expression of faith are again expressed: 'As the body without the spirit is dead, so faith without deeds is dead' (James 2:26). At the same time a clear statement against preferential treatment on the basis of wealth, position or appearance is made (James 2:1–13).

It is here that the way in which the doctrine of justification by faith is expressed in the context of works. As we noted earlier, it is not that works replace faith or are a substitute for it, but rather that faith and works operate together, the one informing and endorsing the other. So we have the illustration of Abraham (James 2:20–24) followed immediately by that of Rahab.

The church must therefore work with the tension of faith and works, applying itself to fulfilling rights and responsibilities in both these spheres. Again, Scripture is trying to prevent the rational mind from tearing faith from works, or vice versa. There is a holistic element to this matrix and the two go hand in hand. Who can determine where works end and faith begins? There is a need for constant monitoring through prayer and discussion as to how effectively God's injunctions are being worked through.

Conclusion

John writes in his first epistle the following words:

> We know that we have come to know him if we
> obey his commands. The man who says, 'I know
> him,' but does not do what he commands is a liar,
> and the truth is not in him. But if anyone obeys his
> word, God's love is truly made complete in
> him. This is how we know we are in him: Who-
> ever claims to live in him must walk as Jesus did
> (1 John 2:3–6).

For those of us who claim to be followers of Jesus and
biblical in our worldview the challenge is evident. We
must develop a lifestyle which truly reflects the heart of
God, as revealed through the life and work of Jesus
Himself and through the pages of the Bible.

I believe this will be through incremental steps as we
make discoveries about God, ourselves and our
communities. God only requires us to walk in the good of
what we have ourselves comprehended. So the starting
point for each of us is not some grandiose project, but a
personal step taken in faith towards a practical outcome.

In the final lines of this chapter I have reproduced the
experiences of a friend who, having torn the ligaments in
his knee, was forced to ride around in a wheelchair for
five days. These five days opened a window into a world
where thousands of people spend all their days. I believe
for James this opportunity provided a means for his
horizons to be extended and his understanding
expanded. In the light of this new-found knowledge he is
forced to take an incremental step towards realising
God's heart for those with disabilities. He is, on his own
admission, a fuller person as a result and carries
something more of God's heart than before the accident.

James Sharp is part of Revelation church oversight
team and a congregational leader in Revelation church in
Bersted. This is a report James wrote for our Disability

Awareness Day after a recent experience in a wheelchair, having torn a cartilage in his knee over Easter.

The overriding thing I felt was a sense of utter frustration at being so dependent on other people. Obviously we all like to feel that other people are 'there' to help us, but when you have no option you feel as if you, as a person, no longer have any sort of self-existence . . . and I was only in the chair for five days!! I knew I would be out of it relatively quickly.

It sounds utterly trivial, put badly on paper, talking of 'how I felt' when every time I wanted to get over an unmountable kerbstone (they might as well have been six foot high, rather than six inches) I had to ask for assistance, but there and then I felt I was imposing on people. I felt stupid and inadequate because I couldn't do it by myself, and I felt as if I was generally getting in everyone's way at times (which I guess I was!!) The point is, though, who has to adapt? Of course *I* did, and those I was sharing a room with did brilliantly . . . but on a broader level it made me realise that *society as a whole*, not simply the person with the disability, needs to adapt, in terms of attitude as well as facilities—however temporary it may be.

I was actually at a Butlin's holiday site when my accident and confinement to a wheelchair occurred, and it was startling that the only concession to disability I came across was a ramp in just one venue. This got me inside the club all right, (although once I was in there I couldn't go anywhere because of the many flights of steps) but coming out was a nightmare—the ramp was so steep that I was unable to control my rapid acceleration, and very nearly made a significant contribution to the emasculation of the doorman, who looked as if he wanted to upend my chair and send me down the nearby water chute for being such a buffoon. I admit that I didn't actually talk to a representative of the Butlin's management, but the entire layout of the site and the 'ease' with which I got around communicated one message loud and clear: 'Wheelchairs are not welcome. This is a pleasure site and you are jeopardising the pleasure of the majority.'

Being six foot four inches tall I am un-accustomed to my head being at everyone else's groin level—in fact I have never (at my present height) met such an enormous human being. In a wheelchair, you not only have to contend with the fact that the first thing you notice about someone is their crutch, but you also feel like a child going into a sweet shop, sheepishly requesting sixpennyworth of pick 'n' mix. How was I supposed to relate sensibly to someone behind a shop counter tower-ing over me like a disapproving school teacher?

Then of course when people do come and give you some attention, you automatically wonder if they are doing it to be nice, to be politically correct, because they feel they ought to, or because they feel sorry for you. I am generally a 'secure' person so I guess that these questions were probably based more on cynicism than insecurity; having said that I have not had to deal with fundamental questions like that since I was a small boy!

It never occurred to me that someone propelling themselves along in a wheelchair feels so isolated. (Maybe these feelings abate with time and experience, maybe they don't.) I felt clumsy too: the camber on the road to provide drainage was so steep that I kept colliding with the kerb. On one occasion I actually thought I wouldn't manage to get back to my chalet at all! Being carried up and down long flights of stairs was terrifying! I must admit that I never realised that it could be too much of a problem getting carried into a meeting on a regular basis, but my feelings regarding meeting venues above ground-floor level have changed somewhat; there's no way I'd want to go through that every week! I believe it goes back to what I was saying earlier about adaptation—often we expect the person with the disability to adapt, whereas surely it must be up to us all to adapt, even if it means hiring a different building.

A few years ago I was pushing a guy I knew who had AIDS to a pub in North London. Outside the pub had a very attractive 'olde-worlde' cobble-stone terrace. I didn't realise it would have been somewhat appropriate to break my stride, preferably skirting around said terrace, rather than persevering headlong at breakneck speed. Nick (the guy in the chair) had every bone set on edge, all his tubes and attachments must have dislodged and all in all he felt pretty cheesed off about my treating him like a meat waggon. I have often joked about this when doing countless lessons in school about 'people I have known with AIDS' etc. Not until recently have I really appreciated how Nick would have felt. I can't exactly go back and talk this through with him because he is dead. However, this has been a good learning exercise for me, and invaluable experience in terms of my ongoing development as a leader. For I too now know what it is like to be unable to respond to the weekly clarion call from our leaders: 'Let us all stand and worship God . . . '

James Sharp

PART TWO

EMPOWERING

CHAPTER 4

EMBRACING THE ISSUE: RENEWED MINDS

The previous chapters may well have raised some serious questions about our understanding of Scripture. Is the Bible really so committed to the marginalised? Surely Jesus did not preach and teach a form of hybrid communism.

Worldview

I believe the real problem in such an approach to Jesus' teaching lies in the fact that we are so shaped by the environment in which we find ourselves. Our upbringing, the way we have been taught Scripture, our peer group and many other factors all go to create an understanding of the world in which we live. This understanding, or worldview, is all absorbing. It is largely subconscious, but determines our outlook on the whole of life.

More worrying is the fact that we normally accept the information from our worldview without question. Thus things which apparently conflict are dismissed instantly, when perhaps a moment's consideration might prove constructive and present a humbler approach.

Our worldview carries all our fears and prejudices, our likes and dislikes, our sense of right and wrong. Unless we are in touch with our worldview we shall remain incapable of fulfilling Christ's command to be salt and light; in other words true disciples.

Let me illustrate. Walking with my mother to primary

school we had to pass by a special school. This, it was explained to me, was for children with disabilities. Most mornings there would be a large green vehicle disgorging wheelchairs with children with a variety of physical difficulties. Something within me recoiled. I could not handle it. From that point on, I guess I made a decision to avoid disability.

Imagine my confusion and distress when in our congregation one Sunday I spied a young man in a wheelchair, obviously with a serious disability. I can remember, as clear as a bell, something within me saying: 'Well, what are you going to do now? Retain your avoidance strategy which has served you so well all these years, or confront your own fear and prejudice?'

Obviously the Christian thing to do is to follow the latter course. But life is not so clear-cut. I had to battle with myself and confront my prejudice. This I did and that day God met me in a remarkable way. I have often recounted this story, for it is so vivid to me and I am grateful that Dick was able to minister to me so powerfully that day, just by being himself.

One of the most telling verses in Scripture is found in Romans 12:1–2:

> Therefore, I urge you, brothers, in view of God's mercy, to offer your bodies as living sacrifices, holy and pleasing to God—this is your spiritual act of worship. Do not conform any longer to the pattern of this world, but be transformed by the renewing of your mind. Then you will be able to test and approve what God's will is—his good, pleasing and perfect will.

Here Paul reminds his readers of their calling. This is to act as living sacrifices and to be renewed in their thinking. In coming to Christ and entering His kingdom we must all learn to abide by its rules. There is a biblical worldview which is the correct view for the followers of Jesus.

The great challenge for the church is to think as Jesus

thinks, not as contemporary society thinks. For this to happen a whole process of unlearning needs to precede a Christian learning process. However, these two processes generally happen together. Each of us is unlearning at the same time as learning afresh. No wonder there is so much confusion within the church, in fact a whole spectrum of views, positions and opinions. So long as we are able to establish these as biblically legitimate, there is no real cause for concern. However, a good deal more charity would not go amiss. If this were combined with open discussion then as a church we might learn effectively from each other.

Thought and action

The importance of understanding and considering our worldview is essential. How we think determines how we act. Our lifestyle choices, perspectives of different people groups, etc. will be determined by our mindset. The mind is the greatest driving force within each one of us. Hence the injunction to allow our minds to be renewed.[1] It follows that those things we are committed to are the things we think are important. Enter anyone's personal world and you can discover a great deal about them by the priorities upon which they order their lives. It is these factors which Jesus described as fruit—fruit which provides an insight into the nature of the disciple's life.

Tension is created for each of us at this point. Honesty in the reality of priorities is hard to come by. It is at this level that we most certainly require the support and advice of others, to prevent us rationalising various non-biblical and unbiblical behaviour patterns as acceptable. This is the battle for the mind—resisting being conformed for the sake of mind renewal.

At a light-hearted level, I still find in my travels that

---

1. See the Pioneer *Perspective* entitled *Your Mind Matters* by Chris Seaton (Nelson Word, 1993) for a full treatment of this urgent issue.

there is an unspoken pressure to put on shirt and tie to attend plenary meetings at Christian conventions around the world, more especially so if one is to speak. Why is this? Styles of meetings also get formalised into a rigid cultural norm which no one can break away from.

Perhaps, more seriously, the pursuit of professionalism in the name of excellence, where professionalism is primarily defined for us by the TV medium which surrounds us, should cause us greater concern than it does; or again, the high-pressured, busy lives which have become synonymous with evangelical leadership and which are in need of serious critique.

The question which should be constantly on all our lips is: 'How would Jesus have us live? . . . think? . . . act?'

Culture and community

Travel throughout the UK and you will pass through various cultures—mining communities, stockbroker belts, inner city sections, suburbs. The list is endless. You will also hear people describing others and perhaps themselves as 'working class' or 'middle class'. Whatever such terms mean in practice, people still use them comfortably to place themselves on society's spectrum.

These cultures shape the community, both internally, i.e. how people view themselves, and also externally, i.e. the stereotypes we develop for certain unfamiliar cultures we observe on holiday or through various sitcoms.

In a broader context, although the UK is made up of a rich variety of cultures there is also a Western culture and an Eastern culture. We speak of 'the two-thirds world' and of 'Europeans'. Our atlases are generally 'Eurocentric'; the UK looks as if it were half the size of a vast continent like Africa. Europe and North America sit on the top of our globes, which communicates a message of dominance and control to folk in other parts of the globe.

At a recent gathering of Arab leaders from the Middle

East and North Africa great hilarity was generated as the globe was turned this way and that so that each contributor ensured their country was uppermost.

These various cultures or 'eccentricities' are conforming factors in our development. Educated in an all-male public school, my initial view of women was a masculine stereotype. I had to have a mind renewal to break free from the conforming process. Growing up in suburbia, certain lifestyle norms were subconsciously imbibed. Hence, when living in Leeds, learning to be comfortable with an unlocked back door and a stream of friendly visitors through it was a challenge. Certain insecurities emerged. Strange and indefinable emotional reactions took place.

All of us are products of this process; and Jesus wants us to realise it and then make a radical critique of our attitudes and actions.

Here is one further illustration. The evangelical church has taken seriously the failure of the family in British society. However, it has generally responded by presenting a model of mum, dad and 1.7 kids as the Jesus style of family. Now in the first instance there is nothing biblical about this model; nor unbiblical for that matter!

Certainly the Bible clearly states marriage is for life, and a stable relationship generates a stable environment. Yet to think in terms of nuclear families as the panacea for all ills is ridiculous. Let us honour marriage; let us encourage effective parenting; let us go for stable environments. But let us not limit God to the nuclear family.

To handle the debris of broken marriages and broken families we need a whole host of alternative models—extended families; networks of supporting relationships; a mutual sharing of financial as well as emotional resources.

It's all too easy to get hooked into one model. Thus blinkered, we then fail to realise that such a model is irrelevant and unappealing to large sections of the very society we loudly proclaim we are seeking to win to the gospel, and who we assure will be helped by God.

In the second instance we are in danger of allowing the voice of the nuclear family to control the agenda of the church—activities for kids; meetings arranged around family timetables; teaching aimed at the typical nuclear family; illustrations always relating to stories of marriage, kids and home life.

This totally marginalises all sorts of other member groups of the congregation. Worse still, it marginalises the church from vast numbers of local people who will pay little attention to so cosy an environment which appears totally irrelevant to their experiences of life.

I speak of the singles, the childless, youth, children, the divorced, single parents, those with a disability, the gay community, the aging, to name but a few. The church is never the exclusive preserve of a minority. It is a home for all, developing a culture, a worldview altogether distinct and which indicates its author as Jesus.

Radical

I used the much overworked word 'radical' above. Suffice it to say that what it really refers to is being honest enough to admit personally and publicly that I am a product of a whole host of factors, not all of them either Godly or helpful. Furthermore, it is my intention seriously to criticise all I do and commit myself to allowing my mind to be transformed—whatever that demands.

Again, in an earlier chapter I spoke of incremental steps. This is the path of discipleship. Step by step we move closer to Jesus; all at different points on the journey; each committed to encouraging the other further; ready to challenge complacency with or conformity to the dominant culture or environment.

The radical step God took to communicate with His crown of creation was to wrap Himself up in human form. This was (and remains) the ultimate medium of communication. All other methods have only met with partial success. This step of incarnation enabled mankind to see what God was really like in Jesus.

It is the best method of communicating one's message. Those around Jesus could scrutinise His life as well as listen to His message. They could question, challenge, seek to fault. Ultimately, because Jesus wasn't going to give up on them, they had to make a clear decision; to follow Him, to go off independently or to remain in close proximity, pleased to have Jesus around but not wanting to get too involved.

Incarnation

This process is known as *incarnational*. This simply means placing oneself alongside the people one is seeking to communicate with and living out one's life. The benefit is that the gospel is given a clear context for expression. Words come to life with practice. The validity of the verbal statements is clearly measurable.

For too long, as has often been said, the church has lost relevance for the people it seeks to reach with the good news about Jesus because it is shut up within buildings. Meeting once a week on a Sunday, generating its own culture, it appears highly irrelevant, should anyone notice its existence at all—hence the necessity to live out amongst the communities it seeks to communicate with.

How does a Christian dealing with single parenthood differ from someone without Christ? What is the significance of Christ to personal unemployment? How does membership of the church affect those suffering from illness or disability?

The original purpose of the incarnation was reconciliation. God broke down the barrier of sin between Himself and mankind. Relationship between God and man was made available again through Jesus' death on a cross and resurrection from the grave. The purpose remains unchanged today. If we are serious about this message of reconciliation we must become incarnational in our approach.

Reconciliation often requires individuals to confront a litter of personal hurt, rejection, abuse and fear. Such issues are not dealt with in a moment. Reconciliation restores relationship. For someone whose relational experience has left them bankrupt there is a need to lay fresh foundations. Such foundations can be discovered in an active community of relationships; the church is designed to be one such community.

Jesus reserved some very harsh words for the 'teachers of the law and the Pharisees' in Matthew 23. Those of us with the privilege of knowing Jesus and aware of the final challenge of Jesus to 'make disciples of all nations' (Matthew 28:16–20 and Acts 1:8) must rise to the challenge of and accept responsibility for an incarnational approach for the gospel.

Recently, during a trip to South Africa organised by *Concerned Evangelicals,* it was with great sadness that I discovered the damage done to the gospel by the failure of the white evangelicals to have roundly condemned apartheid before significant political changes had taken place. The lack of white presence in black townships, even at the level of visiting, to build relationships with black evangelicals, was a poor reflection on the good news of which we are the beneficiaries and witnesses.

Easy to point at another country, many would say. However, our own society is littered with examples of the failure of the church to carry the good news forward in an incarnational way. When travelling in different countries I am often asked to explain the situation regarding Northern Ireland and the British involvement of troops. After all, am I not an evangelical leader? And is not the situation a Christian conflict anyway? It is amazing how easy it is to have a clear perspective and simple solutions to other people's national difficulties, but be somewhat uncertain, if not blind, to one's own.

Citizenship is simply one attempt to encourage the process of carrying the good news forward in an incarnational manner.

CHAPTER 5

PLURALITY NOT PLUTOCRACY

The richest resource the church has is its people. So often a very small percentage of this resource is effectively deployed. One reason for this has been a failure to grasp that good news is more than verbal presentations. I believe there are five factors which constitute the good news; I also believe these alliterated headings appeared in another context in a talk given by Paul Negrut, President of the Romanian Evangelical Alliance. I am grateful for the alliteration and trust he will not mind the content and context I have given them in this *Perspective*!

A. **Proclamation:** This is primarily the verbal declaration of the gospel. We are all familiar with it and it is often the way individuals are brought to a point of personal decision about their relationship with God.

B. **Plantation:** This means establishing viable congregations within reach of people where they live. Such congregations live a Jesus-centred lifestyle within the context of the surrounding community and develop lives integrated into the community of which they are a part.

C. **Preparation:** This has two aspects to it. The first is the teaching and training within the church to generate competent leadership and informed disciples. The second is presenting a Christian worldview across society, touching upon every area of life. In this way the church is forced to consider what is taking place in the world from a biblical perspective. It is an essential step in engaging with the society in which we live.

D. **Penetration:** This means entering every sphere of life and work within society. In this way every church member is a 'full-time worker'. It is time to do away with the élitism which has become associated with that term. Each and every individual acts as an ambassador for Christ. Every sphere of society needs a good dose of salt and light. Every evangelical needs the support and encouragement of the congregation to resist the pull away from Christ which so often accompanies this process.

E. **Participation:** This is the role of the believer in decision taking and planning for the life of the community (micro) and society (macro). This is done through business, politics, leisure, social services, finance, education, retailing, voluntary associations, self-help groups, etc.—everything that goes to make up society.

In crude terms, from the above one might tie **A, B** and the first part of **C** together and say they provide the spiritual dynamic. The rest could be said to give the social impact. Taken together you have the good news Jesus spoke of in the great commission.

Traditionally they have become separated, with some people focusing on the first while others invested in the second. However, they belong together. In boxing I understand that one might lead with the right—telling good news—but must follow up with the left—caring within the community. As a good fighter uses both hands, so must we; and we must also be ready to take the knocks and go the distance.

When we set out in Revelation church to explore social involvement under the title of 'Christian Citizenship', one of our objectives was to redress the balance with regard to the common understanding of the word evangelism. Instead of it being synonymous with door-to-door work, streetwork and the like we wanted to recover its meaning to include community involvement.

We also wanted there to be as much of an assumption that social action involves 'me' as there was when the word evangelism was used. Nobody doubted that they should be involved in evangelistic activities whenever announced; turn up for training and get stuck into the event(s). However, social action was altogether a different story. This was for the specialists; some even doubted if it was a part of the evangelical's responsibility at all.

Kindergarten

Early experience taught many lessons, not all of them easy. In the first instance there was a clear distinction between those seeing social action as a responsibility to do good to someone (regardless of whether they wanted that good done to them or not!), and those who wanted to care and enable people to develop their capacity within the circumstances they found themselves in.

The first category reflected the paternalism which so often accompanies the giving of help. We see the problem, design an answer and then do it. We are then upset when it is rejected.

Some years ago I was being given a tour of the great city of Liverpool. It was not too long after the riots which had badly disturbed a number of cities in the UK. As a result the government had thrown money at the 'problem' without taking too much trouble to establish what the problem was.

A number of building projects had been undertaken, including the provision of expensive youth facilities, the problem being perceived as largely related to disaffected young people. The point made to me verbally and by the bricks and mortar before my eyes was stark. Where the local community had been involved in the planning and development of an estate and its facilities, then these remained intact, cared for and enjoyed by the local community. However, where money had simply been made available and building work undertaken without a process of consultation with those for whose benefit it was designed, then there was vandalism and damage all around.

Community is about participation in decision taking. The involvement of people may prolong the process, but it enriches the end result. So often our suspicions of democratic processes have arisen because we have seen them hijacked by those playing power politics. However, the purpose of democracy is to enable everyone to speak and hence shape the product in question.

Again in South Africa, as the guest of *Concerned Evangelicals*, it was challenging to see the process of democracy at work across the townships. Decisions are made by the community; the community elects its representative leaders; many of the key spokespersons for the ANC have emerged through this informal democratic process. A similar process operates within some of the churches there, which is challenging.

Jesus never forced an issue on the basis of decision. Rather He tried to establish relationship. With the woman at the well He participated in conversation and allowed her to make an important self-discovery, which the Bible indicates was life-transforming enough to make a big impact upon her local community (John 4:4–42). On another occasion in Luke 18:18–30, the story of the rich ruler, Jesus is less concerned about forcing a decision than about communicating content, and suggesting the basis of relationship as the way forward for exploring the message He was 'walking and talking', to adopt modern jargon.

Another factor emerged and this was the lack of responsibility when certain tasks were undertaken— failure to arrive at appointed times; carelessness in decorating tasks; a sense that the volunteer was doing a favour. All such attitudes are unacceptable. The model of Jesus was the servant; our call is to follow in His footsteps.

In our early days of exploration in this field we gave support to the local hospice initiative. Our support was minimal compared to the tremendous efforts of so many; yet there was a real sense of community as we all found common cause together. On one occasion when we were asked for helpers at a fundraising event we apologised that due to one of our own events we were only able to turn out a few. The organiser responded with the immortal words: 'Don't worry; at least I know that when you say people will turn up, they do, and at the time agreed. So at least I can depend upon you.' Responsibility and accountability to the local community are essential.

Prophets, politicians and pastors

Throughout this process of exploration and learning together there were heated discussions! Some people tired of the process; others felt it wasn't their 'thing'. Eventually, however, we crudely identified three types of gifting which had become involved. These were prophets, politicians and pastors.

Prophets were those who felt the injustices done to people very acutely. They were passionate in their denunciation of injustice. Theirs was a challenge to the church to address injustice as a primary issue. However, they were not altogether effective at articulating what steps ought to be taken; neither were they principally involved in responding to the challenge at a personal level.

Their challenge could leave people feeling moved by the issue yet unable to respond at any realistic level, and bridges were required to prevent a sense of compassion fatigue setting in: 'I see the problem and agree it is unjust, but what can I do about it?'

As a framework emerged which deployed people, then they were enabled to become prophetic in deed as well as in word. This dimension of prophetic action is essential as we explore the prophetic. Indeed one of the greatest challenges has been to move the prophetic beyond the verbal sphere, through lifestyles that reflect the values we see embodied within Christ, and by taking the time and investing the energy to develop households that reflect in tangible terms God's many concerns in His world.

I believe such prophetic models are essential—forums in which lessons learnt, mistakes made and hardships borne are openly discussed and communicated as both an inspiration and a challenge to the church in particular and society in general.

Politicians found their energy directed towards addressing and seeking to change the structures which maintained injustice. I quipped frequently that all they wanted was to handcuff themselves to the railings at the council offices to make their point.

Again these are an essential part of any effective community action. We cannot condemn something if we are not prepared to work for change. Much of that work will involve the tedious process of gathering factual evidence and constantly presenting it to the decision takers in order to influence a change of policy or direction. Alongside the evidence a constituency of popular support needs to be generated to express the extent of concern on the issue.

Such steps also need to be undertaken with integrity. In addition, they will require dogged determination and a willingness to be misrepresented and at times personally abused.

It is a sad reflection on the church that a few comments of mine on the failure of the Israeli authorities to apply internationally acceptable standards of justice to the Palestinians forcibly moved to the no man's land between Israel and Lebanon, in late 1992, should generate a postbag from evangelicals seeking to absolve Israel of guilt on the basis of theological conviction. Surely God addresses injustice wherever it is found and confronts whoever is the perpetrator.

One reason, amongst many, for the lack of credibility of the evangelical church is its failure at this level to work for structural change, to speak out publicly and act against evil whether deliberate or accidental. Returning once more to South Africa, it is both sad and disastrous for evangelicalism that the white evangelical church has failed so consistently both to speak up against apartheid and to work for its destruction through all the years of black community suffering.

Pastors, finally, are the many individuals who simply want to get alongside people, to befriend and work with, to support in difficult circumstances. These are the community workers, following in the footsteps of Jesus by eating and drinking with members of the local community, developing relationships of care. My descriptive phrase is residents of the community with open hearts and open homes—giving of themselves out of the rich resources they have received from Jesus.

Obviously these are the essential members of the community—knowing what is going on, able to provide or generate support at a moment's notice, available to generate voluntary support groups where appropriate. They form a sounding board for frustrations or local anger, initiating community celebrations and reinforcing the sense of togetherness across the local community.

All three elements are required and need to be closely interrelated.

PART THREE

ENABLING

CHAPTER 6

THE REVELATION STORY

The way forward

As a church we decided to engage in some healthy dialogue over how to carry these understandings forward into practical action. In so many case studies we observed that although there was a strong start, programmes often faltered. The impact on resources, confusion over objectives, collision with other care providers all went to undermine the process.

Again the fascination with product, or end results, so much a part of evangelical life, put great stress on the project and made demands for early, measurable returns. Often a very narrow appreciation of evangelism led to unhelpful criteria for measurement being applied. Measurements *are* required to maintain the vibrancy of any process or programme. However, criteria must be set which appreciate the nature of the church as a mediating structure in society.

The clear conclusions were that objectives must be specifically stated and understood. The sphere of programmes must be defined and limited to a level which resources could meet. A process of informing the wider church was essential. Also, ownership must be spread widely amongst those delivering programmes.

Think tank

The best illustration I can provide for getting going is to

describe what we did at Revelation church. The process is still developing; I guess it will go on maturing, learning, developing for many years to come. Hopefully lessons learned will prove helpful to the wider body of Christ and solid outcomes will speak of the benefit of following such a process.

Initially, those interested in what was termed 'social action' came together. Meeting regularly for around three hours at a time we began to explore what we understood by that term. Recognising that I carried a heavy sense of vision for the process, I refused the chair, my reasoning being I could all too easily dominate and steer in my direction rather than being effectively influenced by members of the group. Chris Seaton took the chair.

One of our initial objectives was to spread ownership wide. There is a great danger that visionaries end up alone and vulnerable. A visionary needs the broader perspectives provided by others. This incorporation of many people enriches the final outcome. It also slows down the process, which is not always acceptable in the pressured times in which we choose to handle so much of our activities.

We adopted a procedure of reading through the New Testament with a view to discovering to what extent it supported our concern for social involvement. Each member of the group took one or more books of the New Testament and wrote a paper on the extent to which 'Christian Citizenship' was addressed within their reading. These papers were presented at the group meetings and discussed before summaries were drawn together. These summaries attempted to synthesise all that the group were discovering. An individual was given responsibility for this synthesis which was circulated for further discussion.

This process took a number of months to complete. One noticeable feature was the confidence level of individuals as part of the group, and the growing realisation that they could read the Bible for themselves (after all, this is why so many people laid down their lives throughout the history of the church), and present a coherent summary. The debating skills improved and a sense of cooperation and team was generated. Some who had never engaged with this kind of written and discussion process found they could contribute effectively in their own style.

These features were and remain an important element in ensuring that the whole process is widely owned.

Presentation

At the conclusion of this study of the New Testament the plans were laid for presenting the concept and intended practice to the whole church. One member of the group took responsibility for designing a series of housegroup materials. These were set to run over a four-week period, with the final session encouraging each housegroup to develop a contribution around the theme of the 'Citizen's Charter'[1], for presentation at one of the 'Roadshow' meetings of the church.

Outlines were developed, discussed and finalised. The themes for the four weeks were:

1. What do we believe and why is it important?
2. What are we trying to do? Whom should we obey? Who do we work with?
3. How do we work across cultures? and a process to set personal goals in the areas of prophetic, practical and pastoral work.
4. Preparation of materials for congregational meetings.

These corresponded to the headings of the 'Citizen's Charter'. This document, which preceded by a long way Prime Minister Major's introduction of the phrase into the everyday language of the UK, attempted to express concisely the heart of Christian citizenship. It was a

---

1. 'The Christian Citizenship Charter' drawn up by Revelation church is reproduced in the Appendix on page 79.

distillation of all the summaries which the working group had produced and was pulled together by two of the group members.

Before starting the housegroups the theme of Christian citizenship was introduced into the church by means of a presentation at a joint meeting. In spite of the worst acoustic environment designed by man, the three people who heard the content were hopefully helped to engage in the housegroups effectively! At this meeting the Charter was also handed out.

The housegroups proved an essential ingredient. Many of the leaders were stretched by the content. A number of prejudices were exposed and challenged. The clear need for an ongoing educative process was demonstrated. Enabling a large body of people to comprehend and absorb a total concept demands time and consistent restatement of that concept.

A further communication feature was introduced at this stage. These were monthly prayer lunches held on a Sunday. They provided a point of reference where friendships could be developed, updates given and prayer invested. The objective was to provide a point of information and participation for those not immediately involved in the citizenship process, yet who carried a real interest in it.

Task groups

The citizenship process now developed a new structure for the next phase of its evolution.

In determining what areas we should become involved in, two broad criteria were employed. Firstly, we had built up a picture during our study together of where there were particular opportunities within the community. These were opportunities that did not enjoy a great deal of statutory investment. Secondly, we reflected on what interests and skills we had already developed within the church.

Four clear areas were identified: the terminally ill,

people with a disability, homeless people and the environmental or 'green' agenda. It was also decided to seek to establish a general helps group which would aim at producing a directory of practical skills available across the church for one-off jobs. These were often brought to our attention by Social Services and we wanted to be a provider of practical support in this way.

A chair person for each task group was appointed and people with a known interest in a particular area approached to be a part of this group. As the title suggests this was the group to address the opportunity in a practical way. It was task-driven. However, this did not mean a myriad of projects and programmes emerging overnight. Each group was also restricted to about six people to ensure it became an effective working unit.

Training

It was evident that certain skills which were not usually a part of the church's teaching programme were needed in this arena. We therefore approached a senior nurse, who also happened to be a congregational leader, and requested that he, together with another nurse, developed an outline training programme. This was felt to be important in gaining credibility through the confidence of professional carers within the area.

This programme was designed to cover subjects such as *confidentiality*. So often within the church we talk freely about personal information communicated to us on trust. This would be thoroughly inappropriate when working in the community. Another topic covered was *reactions and responses*. All of us have a variety of prejudice levels; some we are aware of, some we are not. It is difficult if one of these unseen prejudices is triggered as we are caring. A wrong reaction can so easily devalue the client and rob her/him of their God-image dignity. We also included a session on *community organisations*, giving a superficial orientation of how the statutory provision operated.

All members of the task groups were expected to participate in the training programme. This really became the foundation course for those wanting to work in 'Christian Citizenship'. Alongside each session (the programme ran over a six-week period) time was given to articulating the heart of citizenship and prayer. Considerable emphasis was given to spiritual warfare. We wanted to take the opportunity to militate against the dualism which so often exists between 'spiritual' activism and 'social' activism.

Finally, all participants were asked to contribute financially to the course to cover the costs and also to establish a small fund for citizenship programmes.

Whilst the task groups carried the responsibility for generating, driving and monitoring the strategies, each task group also developed an action team to outwork the strategy on the ground. At the outset task groups and action teams overlapped both in function and personnel, although latterly the two have become far more distinct.

Action teams are composed solely of those who have been trained. During the final training session the trainees are presented with the work of each task group by the relevant chair. At this point the trainees can elect which task group strategy they would like to service.

A significant consequence of this whole process was to ensure that there was enough real activity to involve the action team in. This has not always proved easy and demands regular dialogue with the action team members. However, in real terms the organisational load of any particular element in any area generally guarantees that there is plenty to do if people are happy just to get stuck in, and not be too worried either about profile or about easily measurable results.

Strategies

Once established the task groups set about drawing up strategies. These were mechanisms for identifying what and how the objectives of the group would be achieved.

In some cases the objectives themselves had to be determined, which could take a large amount of time and discussion.

The following guidelines were drawn up and circulated to the various chairs to encourage the development of strategies on the same basis.

A. **Introduction:** A concise summary of the programme.
B. **Objectives:** The reason(s) for the programme and what the expected outcomes are.
C. **Main section:** A summary of *when, where, how,* and *by whom* the programme will be carried out. An outline *budget* demonstrating costs and potential sources of income. An indication of the *training* potential if appropriate.
D. **Conclusion:** Chairperson's recommendation of the programme to the Christian Citizenship Working Group.

These strategies provided the basis for discussion in the CCWG. Once agreed, the task groups were asked to put the strategy into a realistic time frame. Alongside this time frame the budgetary implications were spelt out so that there was an awareness of when and where expenditure would need to be made. Such expenditure was not costed into the overall church's budget and so necessitated fundraising activities organised by the various task groups.

In developing the strategies it emerged over a period of time that the terminally ill group was not going to be as effective as originally envisaged. The reason for this was not the nature of the group or its membership, but rather the unique needs of a particular voluntary group with which it was involved, which proved too extensive for the membership to meet at this stage.

It was therefore decided to combine the terminally ill and practical helps task groups together and rename the group 'Care'. The major focus which had emerged within the community was adopted. This was in the area of respite care. This development highlights the fact that such a process must always be subject to reappraisal and readjustment. All activities must reflect the reality of needs and the competence of the church as a provider of care. Indeed the strategies themselves proved an effective basis for such reappraisal and readjustment for each task group.

Mention should be made of relations with the local Social Services at this stage. Time was taken to introduce the programmes and philosophy of citizenship to the appropriate Social Services across the variety of congregations making up Revelation. It was recognised that there was a desire to work alongside in the provision of care; also to gain a reputation for a professional and responsible approach. Over time, trust was developed and relationships established.

It is essential that good working relationships are developed with Social Services. There may be a measure of suspicion and cynicism to overcome. There again, so many well-intentioned people and groups have disappeared as quickly as they appeared once the consequences of consistent involvement in these issues has become apparent.

The future

At the time of writing the CCWG is looking to develop a new task group. This will concentrate on political action. With increased involvement in such issues as disability, environmentalism and homelessness there is a need for representation on key matters of concern. The favoured mechanism after discussion is to set up a group which aims to develop campaigning expertise, which then acts as a resource to the other task groups as and when appropriate.

This saves each task group from becoming diverted, with all its energies sapped by a major campaign. However, it does ensure the key elements are articulated by the task group, with its sensitivities to the realities of the issues.

It is also clear that there is now a real need for a part-time co-ordinator. Such a person would relate to Social Services and potential funders of programmes. They would also relate to each of the task groups and help facilitate the programmes, monitor strategies, support fundraising activities and oversee resources to avoid duplication.

Conclusion

We have covered a great deal of territory through this *Perspective*, from a clear statement of philosophy, through biblical background and foundations, to the implementation process as executed by one Christian church.

This hopefully represents our whole approach to everything—gaining an understanding, reflecting Jesus and Scripture and then working it out in practice. Beliefs without an evident expression are of little value. Again, as Jesus reminded us, it is by fruit that we recognise true believers.

It is the prayer of all of us who have wrestled with this subject matter and continue to explore what our thinking means in practice, that you, the reader, will consider investing your skills, finances and energies into expressing the love and salvation of God in ways that cross boundaries; and that you will effectively engage with the many image bearers who find themselves on the margins of society.

In order to facilitate this the team at Revelation are putting together a Christian Citizenship pack which can be effectively taught into the local church. The aim is to enable a clear appraisal to be made of the opportunities, potential pitfalls and necessary resources to prove effective in this vital area. Details are available from Christian Citizenship, Revelation, PO Box 58, Chichester, West Sussex, PO19 2UD.

THE CHRISTIAN CITIZENSHIP CHARTER

A Mandate for Christian Involvement in Society

As Christians, being part of society and very much involved in the local community are essential to the way in which we live out our faith. Recognising that the evangelical church as a whole has partly mislaid this truth over recent years, this Charter sets out six questions to help us to refocus our attention.

It aims to equip the church to move from debating the issues to solid action. The clear goal before us is to see our communities 'salted' and 'lighted' with the love of Jesus.

'Citizenship' is a buzz word for the 1990s, carrying a sense that we all have rights and responsibilities. As those who follow Jesus, we believe that there should be something very special about our Christian Citizenship.

What do we believe?

We believe that it is time for the church to unite around our Christian Citizenship. Many Christians who are interested in getting involved in society have been frustrated by those who theorise so much that no practical action ever seems to be taken. Meanwhile, other Christians have put great emphasis on holding onto the purity of Christian doctrine alone. We believe that biblical Christians are those whose deeds match their declaration in proclaiming the good news about Jesus.

Both action and doctrine are important. Doctrine— that is, what we believe—is vital because our beliefs are reflected in our behaviour and lifestyle. For example, if I hold an extreme view of God's control over all things, then I will think that it is pointless to get too involved. On the other hand, if I hold an extreme view of man's free will, I will find it harder to believe in a supernatural God who intervenes in human affairs.

If, however, we believe that it is what we do, as well as what we say, that honours God, we will want to ask the Lord to give us practical steps of action. Our beliefs will determine what we are going for, as individuals or as church.

Further, what we believe gives character to our church. Amos 5:21–24 and Micah 6:8 reveal the mercy, love and realism that God wants among His people. This is echoed in Jesus' parables, especially the Good Samaritan (Luke 10:25–37).

The entire message of the Sermon on the Mount (Matthew 5, 6 and 7) is the proper starting point for us to sort out what we believe. It starts with the twofold command that the Christian and the church should be the salt of the earth and the light of the world.

What are we trying to do?

We believe that God is a creative God. He wants His creation to advance; for each person to express their individuality in different ways and to take responsibility for their lives.

However, the Bible reveals that God also identifies particularly with the poor, oppressed and socially marginalised. In the Old Testament, God measured Israel's heart and righteousness by whether or not they were caring for 'the alien, the fatherless and widow' in their midst. (See Psalm 146:9; Isaiah 1:17 and James 1:27.) Clearer still, the Lord gave the Year of Jubilee every fifty years to cancel out any negative results of sickness, moral failure and unfortunate circumstances (see Leviticus 25).

Therefore, we believe that Christian Citizens must live a life of self-sacrifice, but that they need not and should not give up everything that is good or enjoyable. Christians should not condemn anything which God Himself does not condemn, but they should stand against attitudes which God hates. These include racism, sexism, nationalism, materialism, idolatry and all oppression of minorities. They should give themselves to those who are ill-treated and to empowering the powerless, following the model of Jesus' life.

Whom should we obey?

Along with many other changes over the past thirty years there have been three clear trends in British society. First, there has been a decline in Christian influence. Second, there has been an increase in the number of different spiritual and philosophical ideas which have been influencing society. Third, there has been a retreat of community life and values and a greater emphasis on the individual. Many Christians never engage in social action either because they just do not know where to begin, or because society's problems seem so big and complicated.

We believe that Christianity is unique in its view of creation, suffering, salvation and the end times. The very things which mark out our faith as different help us to get started and mean that our response to problems must be positive. Above all, we have everything we need to act, with Jesus as the pioneer of loving involvement, and the Holy Spirit to give us power far beyond our own strength.

Nonetheless, Christian Citizens must live in the tension of dual citizenship. They must obey earthly governments in the same way as any citizens must (see Romans 13). However, they must also obey a higher government—the Kingdom of God—and this may well produce conflict. They must be ready to face the consequences of their freedom and of the 'clash of kingdoms' which may result. (See 1 Peter 2:13–17; Exodus 1:16–22; Psalm 111:10 and Acts 4:18–22.)

In summary, we must be 'transformed by the renewing of our minds' and not 'squeezed into the world's mould' (Romans 12:2).

With whom should we work?

We believe that the Christian Church is part of society just as humanity is part of the whole creation. Our call to a close commitment to society is Jesus-centred, not need-centred. As Jesus said, 'Whatever you did for the least of these, you did for me' (see Matthew 25:40).

Only Jesus can be our model for this commitment. In His Sermon on the Mount, Jesus lays down God's demand for His people to have an inward purity of heart, whilst recognising that there are immovable moral boundaries. The call is to live after a distinct lifestyle.

The question which we face is not, 'How *much* should we get involved?' This could lead the church to follow one of two extremes. One would be practical, but liberal—getting the job done, but not necessarily reflecting Jesus' radical character and values. The other would be more cautious or paternalistic—trying to reach out, but being afraid of how this might affect us and perhaps imposing our views too strongly.

Rather, we should ask, 'How do we hold onto our God-given moral boundaries without being legalistic or liberal?' We must remember that it is the world *system* and its principles from which God wants us to be separate, not the planet and its peoples, whom the Father 'so loves' (John 3:16). We must be in the world, but not of it.

In all we do, we must maintain our morality with our words and with our lives, and so convince people of the truth of our message. This may be on a one-to-one level or on a national or global scale. However, we must beware of proclaiming the morality part of our message so loud that it drowns out the part about the love, mercy and grace of God. If we alienate the unbeliever the Christian Citizen is unable to be salt and light to that person.

Working across cultures

We believe that God is interested in everybody—He wants no one to perish, but everyone to come to repentance (2 Peter 3:9). He wants all nations to become discipled (Matthew 28:19). There must be no doubt in the mind of the Christian Citizen that God has called His church to minister to all people regardless of race, religion, sex, class or any other distinction. The unity of humanity is only fulfilled in Christ Jesus Himself, in whom 'neither Jew nor Greek, slave nor free, male nor female' has any superiority (see Galatians 3:28).

We must ask God to give us His heart and His view on serving across cultures. We must ask Him to help us to overcome our prejudices and narrowmindedness which may hinder the Holy Spirit as we seek to help those from different cultures.

Working across cultures may simply mean serving someone from a different social background—or it might mean travelling to work in another country with a different race to our own. Let us keep our hearts open to the Lord, whatever the personal sacrifice involved. The Christian Citizen will have a broad view of social involvement and will be willing to step out in bold, adventurous and creative ways.

In the past, the evangelical church has concentrated on displaying an attractive morality and a consistency of belief. At times it has also made the mistake of imposing a domestic culture and class onto people groups of other cultures. We will fail to show the love of God to people if we are unwilling to identify with them and to try to understand how they think and feel. Jesus drew along-side people and they experienced His kindness, mercy and love without judgement.

We must follow this example, and that of Paul who said, 'I have become all things to all men so that by all possible means I might save some' (1 Corinthians 9:22).

Where do I begin?

We believe that Christian Citizenship is for everyone. Each of us has the same rock founding our faith—Jesus who is 'the same yesterday, today and forever' (Hebrews 13:1). We must begin with ourselves.

We have missed the whole point of the gospel if our motivation is not a pure love of God and of our fellow human beings. It is not what we do but who we are that ministers to people.

Jesus washed His disciples' feet to show that He must serve us before we can serve others—this enables us to be the visual aids of His gospel. If, like Peter, we are unwilling for this, we may do more harm than good (John 13:2–11). Jesus wants His church to be an expression of the father heart of God to a world which is broken and bruised.

Each of us has a vital role to play. Our role might be *prophetic*—to speak out in love, in anger and in truth on behalf of those who cannot speak for themselves. This speaking out will motivate the church to take action.

Alternatively, God might call us to the *political* arena to be a voice locally, nationally or internationally. In this way social concerns and changes in the law can be pursued, and other lawmakers influenced for the Kingdom.

Perhaps others of us are called simply to be *servants*. To serve the lonely, the lost, the poor, the bereaved and the powerless in a 'hands-on' way—to be Jesus to them. Of course, all these areas overlap and may blend into one another.

It is our privilege and our responsibility to ask God how we should serve Him and serve our neighbour.

This charter is produced by the Christian Citizenship Research Group of Revelation, a church working with the Pioneer Team. Contact: Christian Citizenship, Revelation Church, PO Box 58, Chichester, PO19 2UD.

ABOUT THE AUTHOR

Educated at Oxford University, Mike worked with British Youth for Christ before joining the Evangelical Alliance UK. He now serves as their International Director and also Executive Director to the Religious Liberties Commission of the World Evangelical Fellowship.

A member of the Pioneer team, Mike is also part of the oversight team at Revelation church, Chichester. This is a Pioneer church and is currently made up of five congregations. Mike is also an active member of the Rustington Sports and Social Club and a Fellow of the Royal Geographical Society.

He has been married to Katey for fifteen years and they live as part of an extended family. His interests include cricket, ornithology and reading.

OTHER PUBLICATIONS:

Praying Together, Mike and Katey Morris (Kingsway, 1987)
Two's Company; Testament of Childlessness, Mike and Katey Morris (Kingsway)
Pathways in Prayer, Mike and Katey Morris (CWR, 1991)
The Engaged Couples' Handbook, Mike and Katey Morris (Crossway, 1992)
'Religious Liberty', Mike Morris (chapter in *Britain on the Brink*, edited by Martyn Eden, Crossway Publications, 1993)

HEALING THEN AND NOW

Martin Scott

This book in the Pioneer *Perspectives* series challenges us to put healing firmly on the agenda of our Christian lives and of our churches. With the rise in popularity of New Age ideas it is vital for the Church to show not only that healing was an integral part of Jesus' ministry, but that God is still healing by the Holy Spirit through Christians today.

Martin Scott has written out of his experience of praying with sick people over a number of years, during which he has seen both wonderful testimonies of healing and great disappointments; so this is a very practical treatment of the subject. He argues convincingly that all Christians can be used by God in healing, but that we must all recognise those whom God has anointed and make sure we facilitate their work.

With chapters on the biblical framework, pastoral issues, the practicalities of praying with those who are sick and the concept of wholeness—recognising that healing involves not just physical problems but guilt, fear and bitterness—this book will prove a useful aid to those who are seeking to see God's supernatural power fully released in our world today.

Catalogue Number YB 9733   £3.99

Developing a Christian World View

Chris Seaton

This Pioneer *Perspective* challenges us to take a look at the way in which most of us view the world and use our minds.

Your mind matters to God, says Chris Seaton and quotes the French thinker Blaise Pascal: 'Working hard to think clearly is the beginning of moral conduct.'

The author has come to the view that one of the real issues facing Christians is the way we think. There are so many influences shaping our minds—culture, education, parenting, friendships and life experiences—that sometimes we do not realise just what is colouring our thinking.

This *Perspective* will help to clear your vision and make you aware of how your mind works. You may not agree with everything you read in this book but Chris Seaton's prayer is that it will sharpen and develop your thinking.

Catalogue Number YB 9732   £3.99

BETTER THAN OR EQUAL TO?

A Look at Singleness

Linda Harding

This three-part study in the Pioneer *Perspectives* series is a look at the significance of single people, both individually and as groups. Singleness as a topic leads to many interesting and varied questions and author Linda Harding addresses the role of the church as the pacesetter, responding to changing demographics and increasing numbers of single adults.

To be single in the 1990s requires faith and an understanding of God's calling and courage to walk in it. This is the decade when the church has an opportunity to be God's provision of prophetic community, with a radical challenging message.

The reader is helped to understand the biblical perspective on singleness. The book stimulates and raises the level of awareness of attitudes and issues relating to singleness and of the needs and potential of single people. It can be used as an aid to envision and equip the church, to help it respond creatively, positively and practically to this significant group of people.

Catalogue Number YB 9729   £3.99

CARING FOR NEW CHRISTIANS

Margaret Ellis

Jesus clearly called us to make disciples (Matt. 28:19–20). In this very practical guide to help local churches care for new Christians, Margaret Ellis points out how inadequate it is for us to sit back and simply rejoice when someone becomes a Christian.

Without denying the power of the work of the Holy Spirit, the reader is shown how to help new Christians build good foundations to withstand the pressure that will beat against them.

Covering such aspects as: how to convince a new Christian of their need for church; how to train and impart knowledge; how to befriend and encourage, as well as an excellent chapter on how to run a New Christians Course, this *Perspective* will be an indispensable tool for equipping the church.

Catalogue Number YB 9731   £3.99

RADICAL EVANGELISM

A New Look at an Old Commission

Pete Gilbert

This Pioneer *Perspective* gives the biblical basis for the theology of evangelism, resting on the contention that God wants to communicate to His people of all time, all of the time.

Pete Gilbert reiterates the words of Paul to Colosse and clearly explains the role of the 20th-century church and its people to 'proclaim the mystery of Christ' with clarity, wisdom and grace.

Therefore the role of the evangelist, as pointed out by this *Perspective* and Paul's words, is to pass on the good news and to equip and train others to do likewise.

The author writes that in the sphere of radical evangelism, plans need to be created and implemented. Pete Gilbert suggests a 5-point strategy that includes commitment, development, research, action and persistence, which are all fully explained in turn, and a handy help to any church wanting to grow in this decade of evangelism.

Catalogue Number YB 9728   £3.99

RELATIONSHIPS— JESUS STYLE

Stuart Lindsell

For many of us, it is in the area of relationships that we feel the most insecure. Relating to God is not too bad, but relationships with people can be fraught with difficulties and misunderstanding.

This Pioneer *Perspective* is therefore focused on a word of instruction that Jesus spoke to His disciples about their relationships together. Jesus, by His words, His lifestyle of love, acceptance and forgiveness, His faith in his church and purity in His relationships, is our great example. Jesus also recognised His own need of others despite His unique relationship with the Father.

This useful book gives guidance to all of us in creating and maintaining relationships within the church. The biblical teaching is logical and here we have a powerful aid to uniting the church by building strong relationships based on love, acceptance, trust and respect.

Catalogue Number YB 9727   £3.99

THE ROLE AND MINISTRY OF WOMEN

Martin Scott

This two-part study in the Pioneer *Perspectives* series is the result of faithful research into an emotive subject: the role of women in the church – specifically in relation to their ministry as leaders. In a topic of heated debate the author has related the role women should play in the light of the revelation of God found within His Word.

The author points out that the Gospel comes to liberate regardless of differing perspectives; it makes us into the men and women God wants us to be. In Christ there is full and equal redemption for all people regardless of race, gender or social background *(Gal. 3:28)*.

So, how can women best be freed to serve effectively as God wants? If there are questions which remain, let us deal with each other graciously, knowing that God is always willing to shed more light where we are seeking answers, which will help us continue to walk in integrity before Him.

Catalogue Number YB 9725

£3.99

THE WORSHIPPING CHURCH

Noel Richards

This Pioneer *Perspective* is a book written as a result of Noel's experiences as a worshipper and worship leader. He writes to help bring insight and practical help, in order that we can come to a better understanding of what it means to be a true worshipper, and of the role of worship in the life of the individual and the church.

It is often too easy to regard worship as being what we do in the corporate setting of a church meeting. Worship, though, is far greater than simply singing songs—it is about us offering our lives as a living sacrifice to our creator God.

The book challenges the church as a body to make changes where necessary. Noel suggests practical methods of blending together old and new styles of worship, wherein worship can reflect the church's vision (or lack of it!). Worship can then be prophetic or nostalgic. Are you ready to take up the vision?

Catalogue Number YB 9730   £3.99